Don't Worry
About A Thing

Also by Erik V. Sahakian

Shadowlands to the Songs of Seraphim

Check Yourself Before You Wreck Yourself

Where to Put the Ladder (co-author)

Follow Me

Out of the Shadowlands

Don't Worry About A Thing

Lessons on Leaving Worry Behind

Erik V. Sahakian

PUBLISHING

Editing: Alicia Evans
Cover Design/Layout: Andrew Enos

Library of Congress Control Number: 2017948966

ISBN 978-0-9852857-8-4
First Printing: May 2019

FOR INFORMATION CONTACT:

Wildwood Ignited Publishing
35145 Oak Glen Rd
Yucaipa, CA 92399
www.wildwoodcalvarychapel.com

www.eriksahakian.com

Printed in the United States of America

This book is dedicated to my wife, Juanita, and my children, Skylar and Maksim, who have walked this journey with me.

Contents

Trust in the Lord with all your heart, and lean not on your own understanding; in all your ways acknowledge Him, and He shall direct your paths.

Proverbs 3:5-6

Foreword

It was the summer of 2006 in Orange County, CA and I was in the backseat of my parents' car when it hit me…an unexplainable, unanticipated, and unwarranted fear that drove me into an uncontrollable panic. My dad pulled into the parking lot of a Wendy's restaurant and my mom screamed to see if I was okay. I remember sobbing, shaking, rocking, and not being able to respond to anything or anyone. It took about an hour for me to recover even to a point of being able to talk to my parents and to try to explain what I was feeling.

This was the first time that my worry had manifested itself in the form of a debilitating anxiety attack—if only it was the last. The months that followed this experience were filled with dark nights wrestling with fear that became crippling.

It was around this time that my family and I moved to Yucaipa, CA and started attending a church called Wildwood Calvary Chapel when I was a senior in high school. I began to serve in the youth ministry, leading worship, but my heart to serve was enslaved by the anxiety that ruled my world in that season.

I can remember going to youth camps and needing to be picked up by my parents because I was ill from fear. It reached a point where I couldn't leave my house after 7 p.m.

because I knew there was an inevitable bout of anxiety that would strike me at any given moment, whether I was out somewhere or in my bedroom. There were many nights I spent curled up in my bed, feeling physically sick and crying for hours, begging the Lord to take it away or to take me home.

I was prescribed medication for the anxiety and it helped for a season, but I became dependent on them. They were a crutch to me for sure. I wouldn't leave home without taking one and I definitely would not consider traveling anywhere without them. They helped me find stability in a season where I felt like I had none.

All throughout that season, I can remember some of the things that well-intentioned believers would say to me, but unfortunately none of it seemed to help. I knew the right Bible verses and I would read and recite them, but I wasn't holding on to them with faith and assurance.

Then one night, everything changed. We had a high school leadership meeting at the youth pastor's home. We ate dinner, had a time of worship together, and then we wrapped it up with a time of prayer. We prayed with great anticipation and expectancy for some of the events that we had coming up and for the youth group as a whole. It caught me off guard when the pastor turned his attention to me during the prayer. He told everyone to lay hands on me and said that the Lord wanted to heal me of my anxiety.

I had received prayer many times for this issue prior to that night, but for some reason this time felt different. The determination and faith in the room stirred up the faith within me and for the first time since the anxiety had started, I believed that I would leave that house changed. Everyone was emotional that night as we linked arms spiritually to fight this battle together, then we hugged at the end of it and we all went back to our homes.

The next day came and went, then the day after that, then weeks and months went by, and finally it hit me—I hadn't had an anxiety attack in months and I didn't even realize it! The very thing that plagued my life for a year had come to a screeching halt and instantaneously was an issue of my past and a significant part of my testimony.

In the book of Exodus, we read about Moses and his brother, Aaron, approaching Pharaoh to ask for the children of Israel to be freed from their captivity. Pharaoh was indignant at the command that God had spoken through Moses and refused to let the people go. That's when we see God's divine power intervene. The Lord sent plagues upon Egypt to sway the heart of Pharaoh into submission, but he was unrelenting in his disobedience.

As I was recently reading through this story, something new and profound struck the chords of my heart. It's something that we read regarding the ninth plague that was sent to Egypt. In Exodus 10:21 we read, "Then the Lord said to Moses, 'Stretch out your hand toward heaven, that there may be darkness over the land of Egypt, darkness which may even be felt.'" As I read that verse, I couldn't help but focus on the words, "which may even be felt."

The description of the darkness that Egypt was plagued with in Exodus 10:21 is a very accurate way of describing what happened in my life when I allowed worry to evolve into anxiety, and even depression—it was a darkness that could be felt.

The interesting thing about that darkness in Egypt is the fact that it being tangibly felt meant that it wasn't just the absence of light that brought about the darkness, but it was something else…something that wouldn't let the light in. We don't know if it was a cloud, a mist, or some other supernatural way to keep out the life-giving properties of the sun, but we do know for certain that the people could not see for three days, and what they felt was absolute terror.

In my season of darkness, anxiety became the thing that kept out the sun. Not only did it keep me from enjoying the life that could be had in the light, but it also became the filter that I viewed life through. It seemed to haunt me on a daily basis and I could not escape it, at least not by any of the efforts I could make in my own strength.

The beautiful contrast between the story in Exodus, and life for those of us who have or are struggling with fear, is that we have been offered freedom from our bondage. The bondage of worry, fear, anxiety, depression, and even thoughts of self-harm. These are not plagues sent to us to try to grant us freedom. We've been granted freedom by Jesus Christ who overcame so that we can overcome these hurdles with the strength of His Spirit.

Here I am twelve years later and I've been set free from the chains of anxiety that once held me captive. Of course, I'd be dishonest if I told you that I never struggle with it anymore. There have been events in my life—from getting married, starting a family, having five children by the age of twenty-seven, to serving in pastoral ministry and losing loved ones—where I feel the oppression of anxiety lurking. The difference now is that when I sense the onset of panic, I point to the broken chains on the ground of an empty dungeon called fear and exclaim my freedom in Christ. I am free from allowing anxiety to control my life. I know now with all my heart that God is infinitely bigger than any of the things that trouble me at any given moment.

One of the passages that was spoken over me in that season of hardship was Luke 12:4-7, which states, "And I say to you, My friends, do not be afraid of those who kill the body, and after that have no more that they can do. But I will show you whom you should fear: Fear Him who, after He has killed, has power to cast into hell; yes, I say to you, fear Him! Are not five sparrows sold for two copper coins? And not one of them is forgotten before God. But the very hairs of your head are all numbered. Do not fear therefore; you are of more value than many sparrows."

In retrospect, I can see that this passage was a thread that kept me going when I stumbled in the darkness. The part that helped me the most was the truth found at the end of verse seven—"Do not fear therefore; you are of more value than many sparrows." I didn't want to admit it at the time, but now I can see that a lot of my issues with fear were rooted in deep insecurity and not feeling valued. These verses became the gentle whisper that continued to sow into my spiritual wellbeing, even when I didn't want to believe it. Jesus spoke directly to me that I am valuable, and that's what I needed to know. I needed to be reassured of the fact that the One who sees value in me is transcendent beyond my greatest fears. He is the One who defeated sin and defied death on the third day. He is my heavenly Father.

Worry is a tool that the enemy often uses to try to disarm the children of God and keep them from walking in their calling. Scare tactics are presented as obstacles to trip over in this spiritual race, but the Word of God and the Spirit of God are our defense, and they help us run with endurance until we reach the finish line.

One of the people, whom God has placed in my life to help me walk in freedom the past ten years, is Pastor Erik Sahakian. We met in line waiting for hamburgers in the summer of 2008 at Wildwood and instantly hit it off. I have had the privilege of walking through a variety of seasons with him (some of which you'll read about in this book) and I am humbled to call him one of my best friends and a brother in Christ.

In *Don't Worry About A Thing*, Pastor Erik speaks to an issue that is prevalent, not only in the world today, but also within the body of Christ. Pastor Erik's heart for God's Word, his life experience, and the wisdom that God has given him make him a great person to write on this subject.

He has spoken into my life some of the most profound and prophetic words in seasons that I was desperate to hear them. I know that this book is going to be the same thing for countless people.

May the God who sets captives free, open your heart and mind to the reality that you too can be set free from the chains of worry...all it takes is faith in His ability to break every chain.

Andrew Enos

Administrative Pastor, *Wildwood Calvary Chapel*

1

Harrowing Experiences

We all know that "punched in the gut" feeling when life throws you a curveball you were not expecting. That happened to me in 2010 when the Lord began to speak to my heart that I needed to sell my business. At the time, I was running my own successful property management business and also working for another company doing inspections of buildings for insurance companies.

I remember the exact words that He spoke softly to my heart...*Next year will be your last year as a business owner.*

Of course, I didn't know exactly how that would work. The income from my business was hardly discretionary income—that was bill paying money! Still, I sensed this was something that wasn't going to happen overnight and besides, I knew that God had been calling me to full-time ministry. The process had begun. So be it! Little did I know the journey I was about to embark on.

Things Are About to Get Interesting

Now flash forward a year later to New Year's Eve 2011. This day sticks out vividly in my mind. I remember walking up the steps to the office building of a real estate broker who was purchasing my property management business. As I walked up those concrete steps, my arms full of file folders reflecting six years of personal toil and sacrifice, I couldn't help reflecting back on the events that led to the fulfillment of God's words to me just a year before.

The process had taken nearly a year to negotiate and had stalled several times, the longest regarding the purchase price. I was certain that God had called me to sell the business to this person, but he kept giving me ridiculously low-ball offers. We eventually hit a wall that I was not willing to ignore.

I remember sitting in the office of a good pastor friend of mine named, Jason, and sharing with him my predicament. I love how God will often use other people in our lives to point things out with perfect clarity. I remember after sharing the story with Jason, he simply said, "Who knows? You may end up giving your business away." What? At the time, I remember thinking, *Who gives their business away?* Famous last words.

Jason's words haunted me for days. Why did I have such a strong negative reaction to even the thought of giving away my business? So I took it to the Lord in prayer and He answered me with two reasons, neither of which reflected well on me. The first reason was pride—I wanted to be paid what I believed six years of my blood, sweat, and tears were worth. The second reason was a lack of faith. Ouch.

You see, I was trusting God in this journey of faith, but I was also hedging my bets, so to speak. Like Peter, I was outwardly stepping out of the boat and into the storm, but behind closed doors I was making sure my shoes could float! The reason I wouldn't settle for less money in selling my business was because that was the amount I needed to financially carry us through the next year. I knew then what I had to do. So I kicked off my floating shoes and hopped over the side of the boat. In the end, I effectively gave my business away for just enough cash to buy my kids Christmas presents.

Out of the Frying Pan

What I didn't expect was no sooner had the calendar switched over to 2012, that God would call me out further into the storm. I remember sitting in church and hearing that gentle voice...*It's time to surrender your job; it's time to go.* This was a hard one to swallow. I had yet to fully see the financial repercussions of releasing the property management business and now I was being called to surrender my inspection job? That would mean we would have no income, no insurance, and no vehicle of our own. What about our mortgage? What about my family?

I was genuinely worried, even scared about the future, but I couldn't get away from His calling; it was like a constant drumbeat in my spirit. Every time I was in church, every time I prayed, every time I opened the Word, every time I spent time in worship, the words would come flooding into my mind...*It's time to go, it's time to go.*

I remember the exact moment I surrendered my anxiety and fear over to the Lord. My wife, Juanita, and I were sitting in church, the worship team was in full swing, and the Lord's constant words were flooding over me as if I was sitting helplessly under a waterfall. I couldn't take it anymore and I broke down, crying. I remember whispering out loud, "Ok Lord, ok. I will go. I will surrender my job." From that point on the drumbeat in my soul ended, but the real journey of faith was just beginning.

I figured the process would take a year since that's how long surrendering my business took. There would be time to plan, to adjust, to acclimate to this new normal. I could start by progressively dipping my toe in to see how warm the water was, then I could slowly immerse myself.

I was wrong—it was over in months. God had far different plans, He was working from a different timetable, and the real journey from fear to faith was about to begin!

Lesson One:

God Commands Us Not to Worry

2

No Worries

(Matthew 6:25-34)

Did you know that Jesus commands us not to worry? He doesn't suggest we not worry, He doesn't recommend that we not worry; no, Jesus *commands* us not to worry. Why does Jesus make such a command? Well, the root of worry is fear and God does not want us to live in fear. In fact, John the beloved, wrote,

"There is no fear in love; but perfect love casts out fear..." (1 John 4:18).

Think about that statement—"perfect love casts out fear." Where does perfect love originate? It can't come from an ordinary human being because I don't know any perfect people who are capable of loving perfectly. Even an adoring parent who is willing to sacrifice for their child isn't perfect in their love. So where does the perfect love that is capable of casting out fear come from? Again, John tells us,

"He who does not love does not know God, for God is love" (1 John 4:8).

God is love (although He is much more than that), He is perfect in His love, and He is perfecting us through His love! We, as His adopted children through the finished work of Jesus Christ on the cross, can live in victory without fear...*if* we choose to obey His commands. Which brings us to a vital element in the Christian faith.

It's About Lordship

Jesus didn't die on the cross so we could remain living in fear; He died on the cross and rose from the grave to free us from fear! That's why He commands us not to worry. When we live in fear and therefore worry, we are not living in the victory that He purchased for us on the cross.

Imagine that you were starving and I decided to bring you food to eat. Let's go one step further and pretend it wasn't just any run-of-the-mill food, but the kind that makes your mouth water and your spirit soar—the ultimate comfort food! How silly would it be for you not to eat the food that was delivered? Similarly, apart from Jesus Christ we are slaves to sin and fear—we needed to be saved! So Jesus paid the ultimate price to save us. Why would we not want to walk fully in all the blessings that our salvation has afforded us?

Still, at the end of the day, just like eating the food that was delivered, we have to choose to walk in the blessings and victory that Christ has offered us. In other words, it's all about lordship. Are we going to submit and surrender to God's will for our lives, or are we going to remain stuck in the past, living as slaves to fear and worry even though our freedom has already been bought and paid for?

God's will is clear, but the choice is ours to make. So if you're willing to follow your Lord, your Master (Lord means master), from fear to faith, let's take a closer look at what He commands so that we can glorify Him and live victoriously at the same time!

Therefore...Do Not Worry

In Matthew 6, Jesus is in the midst of His *Sermon on the Mount*, speaking to His disciples about how to live righteously for God's kingdom. He had just taught them about the importance of laying up treasure in heaven and how we can't serve both God and materialism, when he makes the following statement:

"Therefore I say to you, do not worry about your life, what you will eat or what you will drink; nor about your body, what you will put on. Is not life more than food and the body more than clothing?" (Matthew 6:25).

Notice the statement—"do not worry about your life." Do *not*, as opposed to *do*. This is not merely a suggestion; this is a direct command from our Lord. It's also not the last time Jesus is going to make this command. In fact, He's going to repeat it three times between verses 25 and 34. I always tell people that when God speaks, we should listen, but when He repeats Himself we need to pay extra close attention. He's not repeating Himself for His benefit; He's repeating Himself for ours!

"Look at the birds of the air, for they neither sow nor reap nor gather into barns; yet your heavenly Father feeds them. Are you not of more value than they?" (Matthew 6:26).

Jesus draws the contrast between the value of the birds and the value of mankind. Of course, He isn't saying that mankind is the only part of God's creation that has value to

Him. All creation, all life has value to God. In fact, Jesus said of those very same birds in the air,

"Are not two sparrows sold for a copper coin? And not one of them falls to the ground apart from your Father's will" (Matthew 10:29).

So God is intimately involved even in the lives of the birds, as He is in ours, yet we have more value to Him than they because we are created in His image.

The point that Jesus is making in verse 25 is that if God cares for and meets the needs of even the birds, which He clearly values, how much more will He meet our needs? It's a rhetorical question with an obvious answer—if He meets the needs of the birds, He will meet our needs even more so!

What the Doctor Didn't Order

Jesus then asks another interesting question:

"Which of you by worrying can add one cubit to his stature? (Matthew 6:27).

A cubit was a length of measurement. One view of what Jesus was saying is essentially can we make ourselves taller by worrying? Of course, the answer is no. However, the more common view of this question has to do with the Greek word, *helikia*, which is translated here as "stature." *Helikia* means "maturity" and can refer to size, but more commonly it refers to age. So the question Jesus most likely was asking is can we make our lives longer by worrying? The answer to that question we know is a definite no!

Medical research has actually shown a negative correlation between stress and the longevity of life, as well as health in general. Worry and anxiety can contribute to high blood pressure, heart disease, poor eating habits, poor sleeping habits, headaches, depression, and even skin conditions. It's fascinating that science has only just realized what God's Word has stated for thousands of years:

"...do not fret—it only causes harm" (Psalm 37:8).

There are many reasons why God does not want us to worry and this is just a practical one—worrying is bad for our health. Nothing good comes from worrying. It certainly doesn't add to the length of our lives and it might even shave some years off!

Why Do We Worry?

Earlier, it was noted that worry is based in fear, but what is fear based on? Jesus addresses this in the next section of verses:

"So why do you worry about clothing? Consider the lilies of the field, how they grow: they neither toil nor spin; and yet I say to you that even Solomon in all his glory was not arrayed like one of these. Now if God so clothes the grass of the field, which today is, and tomorrow is thrown into the oven, will He not much more clothe you, O you of little faith?" (Matthew 6:28-30).

Again, we see Jesus refer to God's provision of the needs of the natural world around us—He feeds the birds, He clothes the lilies—the implication being how much more so will He feed and clothe us.

Notice, in verse 28 Jesus asks the question: "Why do you worry?" He answers the question in verse 30: "O you of little faith." We can all relate to this one—the basis for our fear is essentially a lack of faith.

Now, don't beat yourself up too badly because we're all in great company here. You see, even the disciples who spent each day with Jesus still struggled with this one!

Fear Factor

In Matthew 8:23-27 we read the account of the disciples being with Jesus in a boat on the Sea of Galilee, when a great storm suddenly arose and the boat began to fill with water. Jesus wasn't overly concerned—He was asleep!

"Then His disciples came to Him and awoke Him, saying, 'Lord, save us! We are perishing!'" (Matthew 8:25).

We need to understand that the disciples weren't just merely scared, they were completely terrified! The Greek word translated as "perishing" is *apollumi* and it means "to fully destroy." In other words, the disciples were saying, "Wake up Jesus! We're done, we're toast, game over! We are about to be completely destroyed!" Have you ever felt like that?

There are numerous times in all our lives where we may feel like we are standing on the precipice of destruction. It might even feel like we are alone, as if Jesus is napping on the job.

Yet, look what happens next:

"But He said to them, 'Why are you fearful, O you of little faith?' Then He arose and rebuked the winds and the sea, and there was a great calm" (Matthew 8:26).

The Bible doesn't say what Jesus did immediately after He calmed the tempest, but since He was so rudely woken up, He probably went right back to sleep!

What appeared as a life-threatening event for the disciples was in actuality a minor speed bump for Jesus. We all need to learn not to completely trust our perception of reality. Our information is limited at best or completely false at worst. We are all trapped by time and space, living one moment at a time, but God is not limited by any of these things. We're finite, God is infinite; we're at one place at a time, God is everywhere at once (omnipresent); we know what we know at any given moment, God already knows everything there is to possibly know (omniscient); we're weak and fragile, God is all powerful (omnipotent)—whose perspective do you think is more accurate and trustworthy, His or ours?

That's why we're told in Proverbs:

"Trust in the Lord with all your heart, and lean not on your own understanding; in all your ways acknowledge Him, and He shall direct your paths" (Proverbs 3:5-6).

Why are we not to lean on our own understanding? Because we really don't know what's going on. But the great news is that we know who does! That is why we need to trust in God and not in ourselves.

Now, back to the disciples who were just saved from the storm, did you catch what Jesus said to the disciples in Matthew 8:26? He asked why they were fearful, then He said, "O you of little faith." Interestingly, this is the exact same statement Jesus makes back in Matthew 6:28 and 30 when He asks the disciples, "Why do you worry? O you of little faith." Do you see how worry and fear are actually evidence of our lack of faith?

It's encouraging for us to see that the disciples didn't fully master this lesson the first time out either. Praise God for His grace and mercy!

Spirit of Fear or Spirit of Fearlessness?

One last thought on this issue of fear before we get back into Matthew 6. Remember, Paul wrote to Timothy,

"For God has not given us a spirit of fear, but of power and of love and of a sound mind" (2 Timothy 1:7).

The bottom line is that a spirit of fear does not come from God. Use your imagination as to where it does come from! We do not have to accept a spirit of fear into our lives. As stated previously, it's a choice we have to make—sometimes daily. Satan will always attempt to overstep his boundaries because that's his nature. We can't make him stop being rebellious, but we certainly don't have to buy what he comes to sell. When a spirit of fear comes knocking, we don't have to open the door.

So if a spirit of fear is not from God, did you notice what He *did* give us? He gave us a spirit of "power."

The Greek word translated as "power" is *dunamis* which is where we get the words "dynamite" and "dynamic" from. This is the same word used when the resurrected Jesus said to His disciples, right before He ascended into heaven,

"But you shall receive power when the Holy Spirit has come upon you..." (Acts 1:8).

God has given us the Holy Spirit to lead the Christian in a life of power, not fear. We already have everything we need to live victoriously through Christ because the Holy Spirit dwells within us. Paul reminds us,

"...do you not know that your body is the temple of the Holy Spirit who is in you, whom you have from God..." (1 Corinthians 6:19).

So when Satan comes selling his lies, we don't need to believe them. We can leave the "no solicitors" sign out on the door of our heart and mind. Satan wants to convince us that we are victims, but God's Word is very clear that in Christ we are victors! We don't need to live in fear because as Jesus said,

[37]

"These things I have spoken to you, that in Me you may have peace. In the world you will have tribulation; but be of good cheer, I have overcome the world." (John 16:33).

Satan is the "father of lies" (John 8:44) and Jesus is "the way, the truth, and the life" (John 14:6). Who are you going to choose to believe?

The Second "Therefore Do Not Worry"

Back to Matthew 6, Jesus has already commanded His disciples "do not worry" and He has given them examples of how God feeds the birds of the air and clothes the lilies of the field, both of which, though they have significant value, do not have more value than a person created in the image of God. Jesus points out that worrying does not add to the length of our lives and He also reveals that the true issue of the heart when it comes to fear and worrying is a lack of faith.

In teaching, once the truth has been presented and the point has been made, there needs to be a clear application of what to do with the valuable information that has been given. Otherwise the information merely remains in the head, but God wants it to transform your heart as well, so that it will manifest itself through your life. So what is the application that Jesus concludes with?

"Therefore do not worry, saying, 'What shall we eat?' or 'What shall we drink?' or 'What shall we wear?'" (Matthew 6:31).

Jesus' conclusion is clear: "Do not worry." Notice, He repeats Himself using the same phrase for the second time in this text. In other words, based on the information that we have been given, Jesus is telling us there is no need for us to worry about the basic necessities of life. He emphasizes that point by repeating it twice!

Broken Toys and Unpaid Bills

There is another statement here in this text that should also be extremely reassuring:

"For after all these things the Gentiles seek. For your heavenly Father knows that you need all these things" (Matthew 6:32).

God is not oblivious or dismissive of our needs in this physical world. God is aware of what we need, He *knows* what we need, and He cares about our needs.

Remember back to the disciples in the midst of the storm in Matthew 8:23-27. Jesus was sleeping, fully at rest in the midst of the storm because He knew the storm couldn't hurt Him or the disciples who were with Him on the boat. But when the disciples panicked and woke Him up, what did Jesus do? He calmed the storm. I'm certain Jesus didn't calm the storm because the storm needed to be calmed; He calmed the storm because the disciples needed to be calmed!

As a father, my children come to me with their problems. Some of those problems may be serious, others not so serious. My seven-year old son might bring me a broken toy to fix right in the midst of me trying to figure out how to pay the monthly bills when we are short on funds. Do I dismiss him simply because I'm dealing with a serious problem and he isn't? Of course not. My son's broken toy, though in my estimation is not as serious as paying bills, is nonetheless serious to him in his estimation, and therefore matters to me *because I love him.*

I don't think God is comparing our needs with other people's needs, or comparing the severity of our problems with other people's problems. It's true that not all situations are equal and we may be panicking in a storm that we think is about to destroy us, when in fact it isn't. But because God loves us so deeply, our needs matter to Him. Remember, Jesus said,

"Or what man is there among you who, if his son asks for bread, will give him a stone? Or if he asks for a fish, will he give him a serpent? If you then, being evil, know how to give good gifts to your children, how much more will your Father who is in heaven give good things to those who ask Him!" (Matthew 7:9-11).

God may not answer our prayers the way we expect Him to, or sometimes even want Him to, but don't ever think even for a moment that He doesn't care or doesn't know what we need. He knows what we need better than we even know what we need, and He loves us so much that it will take eternity for us to even begin to understand and experience His love. Don't doubt His goodness or His involvement in your life; instead, believe!

Seek First the Kingdom

As with so many things in the Christian life it comes down to perspective and priority. In this case, a temporal perspective and fleshly priorities versus an eternal perspective and God's priorities. Though our needs are certainly real and as stated previously, God genuinely cares about our needs, the truth is that in order to overcome fear and worry in our lives we need to stop focusing inwardly on ourselves and start focusing upwardly on God.

Remember, the paradigm of heaven and the paradigm of the world are contrary to one another. The world says to focus on yourself to ensure your needs are met, but God doesn't tell us to focus on ourselves—He tells us to focus on Him! That's why Jesus continued on to say,

"But seek first the kingdom of God and His righteousness, and all these things shall be added to you" (Matthew 6:33).

What "things shall be added"? Those needs that God is fully aware are necessary for life. But again, notice those needs aren't met by us striving and chasing after them, but by seeking after God.

There is such peace in focusing on God and not on ourselves. When we focus on problems, when we have that temporal, fleshly perspective, worry abounds. But when we focus on heaven, when we focus on all the promises God has given us, our problems seem less severe because everything temporal diminishes in the context of God and eternity!

That's why whenever I feel overwhelmed by problems and I sense worry about to set in, one of my favorite things to do is go outside at night, look up at all the stars in the sky, and praise God for His greatness. It's hard to stay overwhelmed by my problems when I consider how massive the expanse of the universe is and that my God, my best friend, holds the entire universe with all its stars and planets together. If He can manage that, He can certainly manage the events of my life!

When we seek first the kingdom of God, when we live for kingdom purposes, when we keep our eyes on our Savior, when we hold fast to His promises, it's only inevitable that peace will flood over our worries in light of the glory of the Prince of Peace! And as we keep our eyes on Jesus, our true provider, and not on our ability to provide for ourselves, we allow the opportunity to receive His blessing and provision in powerful and even miraculous ways!

The question we all need to ask ourselves is: do we trust God and His Word, or the broken, failed methodology of the world?

The Final "Therefore Do Not Worry"

Jesus concludes with this third and final command,

"Therefore do not worry about tomorrow, for tomorrow will worry about its own things. Sufficient for the day is its own trouble" (Matthew 6:34).

Life is certainly full of trouble, isn't it? Even Jesus said so. Nonetheless, He commands us not to worry about it. Why? Because ultimately He is in control and we are not. What's the point of worrying about what problems may come tomorrow? After all, there's nothing we can do about it. Tomorrow is in God's hands, not ours.

Three times in Matthew 6:25-34 Jesus commands us, "Do not worry." I think His reasoning and His point are crystal clear, but as it was stated at the beginning of this chapter, it all comes down to lordship. We know what God wants for us, we know what he commands, but are we going to choose to submit and surrender to Him so that we can walk in the victory He has already provided?

It's a journey, a process for each one of us, and no one on this side of eternity has fully arrived yet, but I pray that each of us can answer with a resounding "yes!" that we're willing to trust in God and not in ourselves. Let's be willing to seek after His kingdom and not our own, to stop worrying and start believing, so we can move from fear to faith, from worry to wonder, from fearful to fearless!

3

Tumbleweeds and an Old Rugged Cross

So there I was—kneeling at the foot of the cross. Years before our church, Wildwood Calvary Chapel, had a building to worship in, we had a plot of 16 acres of vacant land. There was nothing on the land except some tumbleweeds, ground squirrels, and an old rugged cross.

People from our church would regularly go to the cross to pray. Surrounded by majestic mountain views nearly all the way around, there was a serenity and peacefulness about the location. The cross was set back hundreds of feet from the street and it was thousands of feet from any nearby buildings.

I was having one of those raw moments before the Lord. I had accepted the call to give away my business, then to quit my inspection job, but now I had no income. I was there at the cross to desperately cry out for some divine direction.

Of one thing I was certain—I knew that I was called to ministry. I'd been keenly aware of this calling ever since I was a teenager. In fact, as I prayed aloud, I was reminded of a promise I had made to God over two decades before.

Keeping Promises

It was the summer of 1990 and I had just recommitted my life to Christ as a fifteen-year-old who was now on fire for Jesus.

I remember being at a midweek Bible study at a friend's house. After a sweet time of worship and the Word, we broke up individually to seek God in prayer.

The house was pretty big and there was lots of room to spread out, so I chose to lay down behind the couch which was in the center of the living room. As I lay there, literally on my face, I remember thanking God for all the amazing blessings in my life.

Prior to rededicating my life to the Lord, I had been a dead Christian—simply going through the motions of Christianity. I had isolated myself in my rebellion and surrounded myself with the wrong kind of friends, but now God had blessed me with new friends who genuinely loved and cared for me.

For the first time in my young life, I truly believed that one person could be used by God in a mighty way, to influence another person's life for the better. So in that moment of heartfelt gratitude combined with a renewed sense of purpose, I overzealously (though sincerely) blurted out, "Lord, all that I ask for my life is that You would take me and use my life to help other people, the way You have used other people to help me!"

What I did not expect was to hear the Lord respond back to me, *One day you will be a pastor.*

Now, if I'm being completely honest and transparent about what happened, then I need to admit that was the absolute last thing I wanted or expected to hear. I had grandiose plans of going to USC film school and becoming a famous movie producer. A pastor? No way!

That's one of the reasons I knew it was the Lord who spoke to me that night because it certainly wasn't me! Being a pastor was so far removed from my personal plans that it didn't event register on my Richter scale.

So in true adolescent fashion, I proceeded to do everything other than pursuing becoming a pastor. In hindsight that's one of the funny things about a calling: you don't pursue it, it pursues you.

As the years and decades passed, I never forgot the promise I made to the Lord that summer night, or His response to me.

Conversation at the Cross

Over two decades later, I finally embraced my calling to be a pastor. Of course, I had no idea where or when this would happen. All I knew was that I had spent all those years complicating my life and now God was calling me to simplify my life—big time!

Though I was serving at the time in the junior high ministry at church, nobody had indicated I would be a pastor there. Sure, I would have loved it, but at the time that I surrendered my business and my job, no offers had been made to me—implied or otherwise. I was stepping outside the boat into a storm and I had no idea what was going to happen.

That's what drove me to the cross that day—a list of unanswered questions. I knew that God had called me to let go of my financial security, but what I didn't know was how was I supposed to pay my mortgage? My wife, Juanita, was incredibly supportive, but would she remain so? And what about our children? They didn't have a say in this but they would certainly be affected by these decisions. Would they grow up resenting me or the church, or even worse, resenting God?

These weren't just questions in my head. These were actual questions I was saying out loud when once again, God surprised me with a response—*You can focus on what you don't know, or you can focus on what you do know. What do you know?*

My questioning literally stopped mid-sentence. I realized I was focusing on the wrong things. Sure, there were practical considerations and unanswered questions, but life is filled with unanswered questions. Conversely, life is also filled with answered questions. The difference in perspective was simply a matter of choice. I could focus on uncertainties, or I could focus on certainties. I could focus on questions, or I could focus on answers. I could focus on what I didn't know, or I could focus on what I did know.

I immediately took out my cell phone and began to write down all the things I did know, beyond a shadow of a doubt. I wrote that I was certain in my knowledge that I was called to be a child of God, a husband to Juanita, and a father to Skylar and Maksim. I wrote that I knew I was called to live in Yucaipa, to serve at Wildwood Calvary Chapel, and that I was called to be a pastor.

Then I picked up a rock off the ground and took it home so that I would never forget.

In the months that followed, whenever uncertainty and fear began to creep into my heart and mind, I would take out that list and remind myself of the things I knew.

Over the years that list was eventually lost as I changed cell phones, but I still have that rock to this very day. Written with black permanent marker it says: God's promises, February 14, 2012.

I keep that rock on my bookshelf in my office at Wildwood to remind me that God always keeps His promises.

Lesson Two:

How Do We Deal with Worry?

4

Pull Up a Chair and Let's Chat

(Philippians 4:6-7)

One of the things I love about God's Word is that we're not just instructed on what not to do, but also how not to do it. This reflects the loving heart of God. He gives us the wisdom we need to walk in victory and power. So when Jesus commands us not to worry, He also provides the instructions on how to leave anxiety behind.

We see this in Paul's letter to the church of Philippi, which was a group of believers experiencing heavy persecution. It could justifiably be argued that they had a good reason to be anxious, but look at what Paul writes to them instead,

"Be anxious for nothing..." (Philippians 4:6).

I think it's important to take a moment to look at the word for "anxious." Although the translators took Jesus' command and used the word "worry" as opposed to Paul's word "anxious," in the original Greek they are actually both the exact same word, *merimnao*.

Clearly, this is not a coincidence. Paul, under inspiration of the Holy Spirit, is making the exact same point that Jesus made. In fact, the sentence structure of Paul's opening statement in verse 6 is truly an imperative, which means it's a command. So we can accurately and confidently say that Paul is commanding us not to worry, just as Jesus did back in Matthew chapter 6.

Does that grab your attention? It should! Consider that both Jesus and Paul are instructing us, even commanding us, that we are not to be worried or anxious. Once again, God is repeating Himself, and as I stated before, when God repeats Himself, we'd be wise to listen.

Now consider the word, *merimnao*. Regardless of what English word the translators decided to use, the meaning of the word itself is to "take thought." Interesting. This truly speaks to where worry originates—in our thoughts. And that is where the tools to defeat worry begin.

Not a Last Resort

I'm human. I struggle the same as any other human being. I have a tendency to try to figure things out, strategize, and plan. I like to think that I don't take risks, I calculate risks. This probably all sounds well and good, except for one obvious thing—where's God in the equation?

Ah, right. Remember lordship? If he's truly Lord of our lives, then He has a right to weigh in on our decisions, especially when those decisions relate to scenarios that create worry in our minds. This sounds crazy, but God is actually inviting us to not deal with our problems alone. He wants to take them off our shoulders!

This truth is vividly illustrated in one of my favorite scriptures in the Bible:

"Cast your burden on the Lord, and He shall sustain you"
(Psalm 55:22).

This verse may not appear life-changing at first, until you consider that the word for "cast" here in Hebrew is the word *shalak* and it means to "throw or hurl." Think about that for a moment. We're not talking about a simple handoff, we're talking hot potato, or even better, a quarterback trying to get rid of the ball before he gets sacked. There's a sense of urgency, even violence in throwing the object away. Literally, God is saying, "Throw your burdens at me."

If that's not an invitation, then I don't know what is!

Unfortunately, that's not usually the first thing we do. In our attempt to solve problems and make plans, we barrel forward without taking the time to consult God. He should be our first step, not a last resort.

I learned this lesson during the time of transition from my business to vocational ministry. We had to let a lot of things go which we could no longer afford to keep, including our two vehicles. Fortunately, my mother-in-law allowed us to borrow an extra vehicle of hers for about five years. That was the good news. The bad news was this car looked like it was held together with bubblegum and popsicle sticks.

Well, one day Juanita and I were taking our son, Maksim, to school when we heard the familiar and disheartening sound of a flat tire coming from the rear of the vehicle. Fortunately, his school was just around the corner, so we pressed on and I only looked at the tire once he'd been successfully dropped off.

We indeed had a flat tire, but the reality was the other three tires needed to be replaced as well. Let's just say that if the car were a cat, it was on its ninth life! All the tires were bald and had wires exposed. We were so broke we didn't have the money to replace even one tire, much less four.

After my friend, Matt, who at the time was employed as a custodian at Maksim's school, helped me get the spare tire on, Juanita and I headed home in silence. Once we got home, we just plunked ourselves down on opposite sides of the couch and wallowed in our self-pity, which we did for close to an hour.

Then I noticed there was a text waiting to be read on my phone. It was from Matt and it had arrived an hour before, probably right as we were giving up on the couch. The text said, "Take your car to the tire shop tomorrow...you're getting four brand new tires!"

It turned out that Matt had called his wife Angela right after we'd left him at the school and told her all about what had happened to our car. So she jumped on the phone to get the word out and in less than ten minutes our church family had collected enough money for the new tires.

I'll never forget the simple joy and elation in that moment of celebrating God's generous provision, but I also realized something else in that moment, too, which was far less celebratory. Not only had I wasted an hour of my life feeling worried and sorry for myself over a problem that didn't even exist, but I had brought Juanita down with me. Even worse, I hadn't even bothered to cry out to God.

You see, after commanding us not to be anxious, Paul immediately tells us what we're supposed to do instead:

"Be anxious for nothing, but in everything by prayer and supplication, with thanksgiving, let your requests be made known to God" (Philippians 4:6).

In other words, Paul is saying, "Don't worry, pray." I consider this another "invitation" verse because we're told to "let your requests be made known to God." God loves when we talk to Him, when we invite Him into our lives. There's something about prayer that is not only powerful, but valuable as well, not only to us, but to God.

Telling Him What He Already Knows

There's a fascinating contrast between two scriptures that really illustrates the mysterious value that God places upon prayer.

Remember, back to what Jesus said:

"For after all these things the Gentiles seek. For your heavenly Father knows that you need all these things" (Matthew 6:32).

Jesus makes it crystal clear that God already knows our every need. In fact, I propose to you that God knows our needs so well, He not only knows what we need better than we do, but He also knows what we need even when we *don't* know what we need. I think it's safe to say that most of the time we don't know what we don't know, but God does!

So if this is true (and it is), then why does Jesus say just a few verses later,

"Ask, and it will be given to you; seek, and you will find; knock, and it will be opened to you. For everyone who asks receives, and he who seeks finds, and to him who knocks it will be opened" (Matthew 7:8-9).

Do you see the obvious question? If God already knows what we need, even when we don't, then why does He want us to ask anyway?

Could it be that prayer isn't simply just a means to an end, but perhaps even an end unto itself? It's not difficult to imagine a relational God desiring to spend quality time with His children just for the sake of spending time together.

I love doing things and going places with Juanita and the kids, but I don't technically need to be doing anything in particular with them to be enjoying myself. Some of my favorite moments are when we are just hanging out and talking over dinner or in the car. Is God so different?

I believe God wants us to ask, seek, and knock, not just to have our needs met, but because there is value in the pursuit. He's the ultimate prize.

So it should come as no surprise that God invites us to let our requests be made known to Him. He wants us to communicate, He wants us to pour out our heart. We aren't informing Him of anything He doesn't already know, but we are sharing the experience of life, through an anxious moment, with Him.

You might even say God redeems our trials by using them as a means to foster deeper and more real communication with Him.

An Attitude of Gratitude

Paul addresses another tool to overcome worry in our lives and that is to remind ourselves of all God's faithfulness and past blessings.

It's a powerful truth that's embedded inconspicuously in the middle of the verse,

"Be anxious for nothing, but in everything by prayer and supplication, with thanksgiving, let your requests be made known to God" (Philippians 4:6).

When we bring our prayer requests, our problems and burdens to God, we need to do it in such a way that we acknowledge our thankfulness. When we're going through difficult times this may seem like a contradiction, but it isn't.

Consider the following verse:

"For in Him we live and move and have our being" (Acts 17:28).

Literally, the very animating force that keeps us alive originates from God. We wouldn't even exist if it weren't for Him. Everything we have and everything we are is owed to God. So even when we bring our needs to Him in prayer, we need to balance the request with our gratitude for all that He has already generously done for us.

[63]

For example, let's say that you've had a difficult month financially and you don't see how you'll be able to make your mortgage payment. What would a thankful prayer when you're potentially risking losing your home sound like? Perhaps something like this: "Lord, I don't know how we're going to make our house payment this month. We desperately need Your provision. Still, I thank You that we have a roof over our heads and so many wonderful memories in this home. I wouldn't be praying for provision for this mortgage payment if we didn't have the blessing of this house to begin with. Thank You."

That's what Paul referred to as "prayer and supplication, with thanksgiving." A similar prayer can be spoken over issues related to employment, health, and relationships. The reality is that our God is so generous and loving, that even when we are in need, our blessings far outweigh anything we lack.

This truth can't be illustrated any more vividly than when Paul writes,

"He who did not spare His own Son, but delivered Him up for us all, how shall He not with Him also freely give us all things?" (Romans 8:32).

The greatest need that every human being has isn't paying their mortgage, or who they're going to marry, or even what they will have for dinner. The greatest need is to be reconciled to a holy God because that determines our eternal destination. Which is exactly what Paul is referring to in Romans 8:32. God recognized that need and didn't hesitate to sacrifice His own Son in order to meet that very need. So then why would we doubt that He will "freely give us all things"? If God was willing to meet our greatest need, why wouldn't He meet a lesser one, right?

Which brings us back to an attitude of gratitude. A mindset of thankfulness will always combat worry because instead of focusing on what we don't have we praise Him for what we do.

Furthermore, in doing so we remind ourselves of His past faithfulness, and in a similar flow of logic as Romans 8:32, if He's been faithful in the past, why would we doubt His faithfulness in the future? Therefore, we can say,

"The Lord has done great things for us, and we are glad" (Psalm 126:3).

The psalm doesn't say that God has "done great things for us, and we are worried, or fearful." It says, "we are glad." This demonstrates there is a biblical connection between God's faithfulness and our faith.

The word "glad" in Hebrew is the word *sameach* and it means to be "joyful, merry, or gleeful." All of which are the exact opposite of anxious and worried. You see, thankfulness brings gladness, which in turn defeats worry.

It's interesting because being thankful doesn't necessarily change our circumstances, just how we react or respond to them. Which brings us back to our first tool—prayer.

Prayer Brings Peace of Mind

Is there another reason why Paul tells us, "Don't worry, pray"? Another gift, if you will, besides an opportunity to pursue God deeper?

Once again, we see His generosity on full display as He offers us, through prayer, a practical blessing in the midst of the storm.

So let's take our subject verse and follow it one step further:

"Be anxious for nothing, but in everything by prayer and supplication, with thanksgiving, let your requests be made known to God; and the peace of God, which surpasses all understanding, will guard your hearts and minds through Christ Jesus" (Philippians 4:6-7).

We've all seen people go through life's storms and setbacks with such peace and calm that it seems illogical. It doesn't make any sense—a terminal diagnosis, the loss of a job, the ending of a relationship—yet the person seems calm, perhaps, though saddened by the specific situation, even filled with an overall joy. How is such a peace that "surpasses all understanding" possible?

Well, first of all, it's not—apart from Jesus. There's nothing natural about peace that surpasses all understanding, it can only be supernatural in origin.

That's why Paul says in verse 7 that it's "the peace of God" and it comes "through Christ Jesus."

[66]

However, the real key is what this type of supernatural peace does. Remember, worry begins in the mind, in our thought life. Before we can act worried, before there are physical manifestations of worry (such as lack of sleep, loss of appetite, emotional withdrawal), there must first be the "thought." The battlefield truly begins in the mind.

Connected to our mind is our emotions. The Greek word for "heart," *kardia*, can also mean "feelings or emotions." So it can be said that when the Bible speaks of our mind it is speaking of our thoughts, and when it references our heart it can literally mean the organ or the seat of our emotions.

These are what Jesus was referring to when He said,

"You shall love the Lord your God with all your heart, with all your soul, and with all your mind" (Matthew 22:37).

Therefore, since the mind is the battlefield, ground zero, we absolutely must build up the defenses of our mind. We must guard our heart (emotions) and mind (thoughts).

Notice in verse 7 how this is accomplished:

"And the peace of God, which surpasses all understanding, will guard your hearts and minds through Christ Jesus" (Philippians 4:6-7).

So our hearts and minds are guarded by the peace of God, which is the very same peace that surpasses all understanding. They are one and the same. And how do we get this peace? Let's look at verse 6 again.

"In everything by prayer and supplication, with thanksgiving, let your requests be made known to God" *(Philippians 4:6).*

In other words, we pray. Prayer is the key to opening the door of God's peace which surpasses all understanding.

Is it any wonder why Satan does everything he can to keep us away from prayer? The devil wants us enslaved to worry and anxiety. He wants us walking in defeat, not power. He wants us thinking and therefore living like victims, not victors. Yet, Satan cannot eliminate the tools that God has given us, he can only distract us or convince us not to use them.

Prayer is a powerful tool to counter and defeat those overwhelming thoughts and feelings of worry in our lives. Through prayer we invite God to intimately walk with us through life's storms so we aren't alone. Through prayer we invite God to intervene and bring resolution, through His strength and not our own, to difficult circumstances. Through prayers of thankfulness we're reminded how blessed we truly are and how good our God is. Finally, through prayer He imparts to us His peace that surpasses all understanding and guards our hearts and minds through Christ.

If you're reading this book because you're being defeated by feelings of worry and anxiety today, I invite you to put this book down and take a moment to pray. Don't put it off or wait for a more convenient time. The best time to seek the Lord in prayer is always as soon as possible!

One Last Thought

When Paul originally wrote this letter to the church in Philippi, there were no numbered chapters or verses. So what we read as verses 6-7 was really just a sentence that flowed into what was later labeled as verse 8. It would be wrong of me to ignore this next verse because it truly hits home the importance of what we let our minds (thoughts) dwell on.

Paul writes,

"Finally, brethren, whatever things are true, whatever things are noble, whatever things are just, whatever things are pure, whatever things are lovely, whatever things are of good report, if there is any virtue and if there is anything praiseworthy—meditate on these things" (Philippians 4:8).

To meditate means to truly dwell on, to exercise deep and deliberate contemplation. It's not a fleeting thought that goes in one ear and out the other. To meditate means you linger, you stop and smell the roses.

Notice what God, through Paul, is instructing us to meditate on—things that are positive, truthful, and beautiful. Good things.

We have a choice here, but only one is sanctioned by God. We can choose to dwell on the ugly things of this world, or we can choose to dwell on the fingerprints of God that are all around us.

Worry feeds on itself. It's a vicious cycle of fear, stress, and anxiety, all based on the unknown. I've never known anyone who claimed to feel better after spending precious time meditating on worrisome, negative thoughts. What I have known are people who have done that and felt worse because of it.

We can learn a lot from Philippians 4:8, not just by what it says, but what it doesn't. What do I mean by that? By Paul telling us what we should meditate on, we can infer from the Holy Spirit what we *shouldn't* meditate on (whatever is false, ignoble, unjust, impure, ugly, of bad report, any vice, and dishonorable).

I believe this choice is what God was speaking of when He said to me at the cross—*You can focus on what you don't know, or you can focus on what you do know. What do you know?*

A big part of the battle for our mind is what we put in our mind, what we expose ourselves to, and what we dwell on. If we want our hearts and minds to be guarded by peace in Christ, we need to be active partners and make wise choices. Are we working with God to secure the battlefield, or are we sabotaging His efforts and aiding the enemy?

The answer to that million-dollar question is strongly worth consideration.

5

What Can You Lose?

Later in the spring of 2012, not long after that powerful moment at the cross, I was having lunch with one of the Wildwood pastors and I was sharing with him some of my very real worries and fears. After patiently listening to me, he asked me a thought-provoking question, "What's the worst thing that could happen to you?" I paused for a moment to consider the possible consequences of my decisions.

What I didn't know then, but would learn in the coming year, is that my decision would cost us our retirement, good credit score, deplete our savings, jeopardize our home, cost us our vehicles, and place us in debt. At the time though, all I could imagine was our struggling to meet our biggest expense—our house.

So I answered his question, "We could lose our house."

He thoughtfully considered my answer, then he replied, "Will you be homeless?"

"No," I said, "I'm sure we could afford an apartment somewhere in town."

"So what have you really got to lose?" He smiled. "The worst that will happen to you is you'll have to move. It's not like you've made a life or death decision."

The shocked look on my face made him laugh!

"Think about it," he said, "it's not like you're headed towards uncharted territory. You're stepping out in faith and taking a chance like many have done before you. The Bible is filled with examples of men and women who had more to sacrifice and lose than you do."

I suddenly felt very silly because I realized he was right. I was definitely not a trailblazer. My venture of faith wasn't really that dramatic, historically speaking. Don't get me wrong, it was very real to us and our faith would be stretched in ways that we could never have imagined, but we weren't alone, we were in great company. Truthfully, we were only risking our comfort and convenience.

I left the meeting feeling very uplifted and encouraged. It truly helped me to have our experience placed in a much larger context, beyond ourselves. Looking back at God's faithfulness, it's hard not to smile.

Riding the Roller Coaster

Around that time, I was invited to come on staff at the church, not as a pastor, but as an editor. I was budgeted ten hours a week at minimum wage. The money was barely enough to buy groceries and put gas in our "borrowed" car, but it was a blessing and a step toward the fulfilment of God's promise.

So we ate out less, learned to shop at yard sales, looked forward to our annual family vacations to Palm Desert (which is a short drive from home), and forgot about Disneyland passes.

Still, in the years that followed, God met all our physical needs. I learned to buy antiques from yard sales at below market prices, then sell them for a modest profit. I taught journalism and creative writing electives at a local charter school. In an exciting twist that we didn't see coming, Juanita was also brought on staff at Wildwood to assist in the women's ministry.

Meanwhile, my responsibilities and hours began to steadily increase at the church. I was asked to oversee the counseling ministry, the graphic design department, and funerals. I remember I had a little two-foot shelf in the office hallway that I used as my desk. It barely had enough room for my laptop!

We learned to live on less, streamlining and scaling back our lifestyle. We cancelled all our subscription services, bought our clothing at discount retailers, and became committed to coupons and rewards programs.

There were so many ups and downs in those years that it felt like a roller coaster. Instead of resisting God's "stripping away" different elements of our past life, I became fascinated to see what we could put on the chopping block next. And in the midst of it all, we laughed and had fun as a family. After all, this was a family adventure, and the kids were keenly aware that something truly special was taking place.

The best part is that we saw miracles take place—so many miracles!

Miracle After Miracle

There was the time our car broke down and my in-laws (who had loaned us their vehicle), told us it would cost $2,000 to fix it. I had it towed to the mechanic and I remember telling Juanita, "Be prepared. We may need to leave the car there for a long time." It was a Friday afternoon, so the mechanic told me he would call on Monday morning with his estimate.

That Sunday night after our weekly prayer service, a man came up, shoved some cash into my hands, and told me God directed him to give me that money. I thanked him and when I got to my car I counted $123—what a strange amount. The next day, the mechanic called and said the problem was that a sensor had gone bad and it would cost $123 to fix it!

Around Christmas, we had no idea how we were going to buy the kids presents that year. I remember Juanita and I having a very frank discussion about it as we were getting ready for the day. Then, as she walked me to the front door as I was leaving for work, we saw a small unmarked box with Christmas wrapping paper sitting on the porch. I picked it up and handed it to her. She opened it and there was $500 inside with a note telling us to buy the kids presents.

And, as expected, we did almost lose our home. In fact, we ended up ten months behind on our mortgage. I exhausted every single avenue I could think of, but each one was a closed door. The nail in the coffin came when a government program, after taking six months to process our application, finally denied us. At that point, I finally accepted in my heart and soul that we would be moving from the home we thought we'd be raising our children in.

Then, in a sudden turn, within a two-week period a handful of different families, none of whom fully knew our situation or even of one another's involvement, all offered to contribute money toward our financial needs. Each was a shock and surprise, but when it was all totaled it equaled exactly the amount we needed to get caught up on our mortgage. The mess that took ten months for us to get in, God took two weeks to get us out.

Many of the miracles were financial, but not all. We had no health insurance, but we never had to see a doctor because none of us ever became seriously sick. The children both attended the same school, and Juanita and I worked at the same location, so we were able to get by with just one car for years. We even read through the entire New Testament as a family on our morning commute!

I could seriously write another book about all the crazy miracles and events that took place in those transitional years that the Lord was moving us away from our former life into a life surrendered to Him in full-time vocational ministry. I should have kept a journal, but I didn't. I regret that in retrospect. I suppose I was too busy riding the wave to give it much reflection at the time.

Promises Kept

All those years, I never knew when, where, or how the Lord would fulfill the promise He'd made to a fifteen-year-old boy, praying behind the couch at his best friend's house. Yet, as the Lord always does, He kept His promise.

On December 15, 2013, nearly twenty-three years later, and two years after I had walked away from my successful property management business, I was ordained as a pastor at Wildwood Calvary Chapel.

Of course, that wasn't the end of the journey—it was only the beginning!

Lesson Three:

A Special Gift of the Lord

6

Waiting with Expectancy

(Isaiah 40:31)

Probably the most challenging aspect of overcoming worry is the period of uncertainty as we wait for God's sovereign and perfect timing. We know from Jesus' and Paul's instructions that we are commanded not to worry. It's never God's will for us to worry. We also know that we have been given supernatural tools to help us combat and overcome worry, such as: casting our problems on Him, communicating through prayer, demonstrating an attitude of thankfulness, and reorienting our minds to an eternal perspective. Which all place us on the path toward victory, but then what? We wait.

A shudder may have just tingled down your spine! Waiting…it's one of the singularly simplest and yet difficult experiences of the Christian walk. Everything in our flesh and human mind resist it. Waiting seems weak, passive, ineffective, and apathetic. It defies our carnal logic and mocks worldly intelligence.

Our culture encourages us not to wait for things to happen to us, but instead, go out and make things happen. Grab the bull by the horns, make your mark, and show 'em who's boss. That's the world's wisdom, but what does God say?

"'For My thoughts are not your thoughts, nor are your ways My ways,' says the Lord. 'For as the heavens are higher than the earth, so are My ways higher than your

ways, and My thoughts than your thoughts'" (Isaiah 55:8-9).

God's economy does not mirror the world's, and His way of accomplishing His purposes is not subject to man's agreement or understanding. Certainly, God does call us to action, but He's the one leading the charge, not us. So when He says "act," we act, but when He says "wait," we wait. That's because He's the Master and we're simply His beloved and cherished servants.

Which is fine by me! God's divine knowledge and understanding are infinite and complete, while ours is absolutely limited at best, and flat out wrong at worst.

Like God told Job,

"Where were you when I laid the foundations of the earth? Tell Me, if you have understanding" (Job 38:4).

The point that God made to Job is clear. *Job, you haven't been around very long. Your existence is literally just a speck in eternity. You don't know nor could you possibly understand what's really going on here. Do you really think you know better than Me?* God's asking all of us that very same question.

I'll only speak for myself when I truthfully answer God's rhetorical question. I don't have understanding. What little I'm able to understand is miniscule compared to what there is to know. I don't even know what I don't know! Fortunately, God doesn't ask us to understand…He asks us to trust in Him.

And that's where waiting comes in.

Wait for It

The word "wait" appears over 100 times in the Bible and 25% of the time it's the Hebrew word *qavah*. I believe this special word holds another key to overcoming worry and also another step of intimacy with Jesus.

We see *qavah* when Isaiah encouraged,

"But those who wait on the Lord shall renew their strength; they shall mount up with wings like eagles, they shall run and not be weary, they shall walk and not faint" (Isaiah 40:31).

So *qavah* produces three major outcomes: 1) renews our strength, 2) mounts us up with wings like eagles, and 3) allows us to run and walk without becoming weary or faint. Who knew that waiting could produce such epic results?

It almost doesn't make any sense. How could waiting produce anything? Remember, the world's view of waiting is that it's passive and equates to inaction. So for waiting to produce results would be like saying something came out of nothing. Unless waiting isn't the same as doing nothing. What if God's version of waiting is profoundly different than the world's version?

This is certainly true when we speak of the word *qavah*. In Hebrew, the nuance for this word, translated as "wait" in English, actually means to wait with anticipation or expectancy.

It reminds me of my children, Skylar and Maksim. When they were much younger, yet old enough to understand that with Christmas came gifts, they would begin to prepare themselves. By November they'd be researching the toy catalogs, making space in their bedrooms, and being on their best behavior. Though it had not yet arrived, they were certain that Christmas was coming. There was no doubt or uncertainty in their minds. They were waiting for Christmas…with expectancy!

That's the kind of waiting that renews our strength when we're feeling defeated and down. That's the kind of waiting that allows us to mount up with an "eagle's eye" perspective of life and its trials. That's the kind of waiting in the race of life, whether we're running at full speed or walking, that allows us to keep going and persevere.

It's waiting with expectancy. Expecting what? Expecting that God, in His sovereignty, will act on our behalf and in His perfect time. In other words, *qavah* is waiting with faith and confidence that God keeps His promises.

Promises such as,

"For the eyes of the Lord run to and fro throughout the whole earth, to show Himself strong on behalf of those whose heart is loyal to Him" (Second Chronicles 16:9).

See, the waiting that God calls us to isn't a passive, sitting around and twiddling your thumbs, kind of waiting. It's not a timid "gee whiz, aw shucks" kind of waiting, as we draw circles in the dirt with the tip of our shoes, averting eye contact.

Qavah is waiting with boldness and faith, believing that God is going to act, He is going to intervene. It's not a matter of *if*, it's a matter of *when*. Like Christmas, it's coming. We can count on it and be ready and prepared for it when it does.

This kind of waiting gives us strength and an eternal-minded perspective that God is in control (and has always been). Whatever the challenges and difficulties that lead our thoughts to wander into the realm of worry, waiting on God reminds us that He is bigger than any trial or tribulation that we face. That's why waiting gives us the stamina to not give up, not give in, and keep moving forward.

It's the power of quiet, meditative contemplation of who God is and what He's capable of. It's the reason why I shared with you back in chapter one that I love to go outside at night, when I'm overwhelmed by life's problems, and just allow myself to bask in the enormous universe that is small in my Savior's hands.

We see this in the psalmist's praise and God's response,

"God is our refuge and strength, a very present help in trouble. Therefore we will not fear...Be still, and know that I am God" (Psalm 46:1-2, 10).

Is it any wonder that Satan does his best to cause us to abhor waiting? He wants us to think that waiting is the equivalent of sitting idly by and allowing circumstances to happen to us, like sheep led to the slaughter.

Nothing could be further from the truth.

Wimps don't wait, warriors wait! Prayerful waiting is not passive, it's powerful. It can give us victory over our feelings of worry and anxiety, and yet, there's another element of *qavah*—a gift that God wants to give us.

Twisted and Bound as One

There's another definition for the word translated as "wait" in English, another layer of meaning in the word *qavah*. The first time I read it I was confused. You see, *qavah* also means "to bind or twist together."

What is bound? What is twisted together? And what does any of that have to do with waiting? Whenever I'm stumped by something in God's Word that I do not understand, the first thing I do (before grabbing a commentary) is go directly to the Author with my question.

I remember praying, "Lord, I don't understand. Please reveal to me what this means. What does waiting with expectancy have to do with binding and twisting? Who or what is this referring to?"

As I meditated on these words, I sensed the Holy Spirit speaking to me, giving me the insight I was seeking. His answer stirred my faith and my heart.

We are the ones being bound and twisted together. I use the season of waiting to draw you closer to Me in deeper intimacy and oneness.

Then it hit me like a ton of bricks! God uses waiting, He redeems it to do a powerful work in our lives. No wonder our flesh resists it; no wonder the enemy tries to stir up our impatience. There's a powerful gift being imparted—oneness!

Oneness is the very thing our Savior seeks. It's what drove Him to the cross. The intimacy that was lost in the Garden was restored at the cross for those who choose it.

Jesus made His intentions crystal clear when He stated,

"They all may be one, as You, Father, are in Me, and I in You; that they also may be one in Us, that the world may believe that You sent Me" (John 17:21).

Oneness is the heart of God and it's rooted in His desire and love for us. No wonder God allows seasons of waiting in our lives. Waiting brings oneness! It's ironic that in the moments when we may feel God is doing the least in our lives, He is actually doing an amazing and powerful work by drawing us together and binding us as one.

It reminded me, once again, that God never lets any experience of our lives go to waste. He redeems it all for His glory and our growth.

Worry, Waiting, and Oneness

It's not a coincidence that the events in our lives that often create the greatest opportunity for worry also create the greatest opportunity for waiting. Worrisome scenarios don't usually go away overnight. They stretch us and test us, and if we keep our eyes on Jesus, they also drive us to our knees in prayer…perhaps over and over again. It's the very season of prolonged prayer that we are often given no choice but to wait.

This is not God being cruel, dismissive, or absent. It's the exact opposite! What may appear on the surface to be unanswered prayer is actually God loving us so much that He is taking back what the enemy intends to discourage and destroy us.

There is a process and a plan that is always taking place behind the scenes, whether we realize it or not, whether we feel it or not.

For example, do you ever stop to think about the fact that you don't feel Earth rotating on its axis? Earth spins approximately 1,000 miles per hour at the equator, yet no one senses it. We see the effects of the rotation, but we never actually feel that we are moving. Just because we don't feel the movement doesn't mean that nothing is happening!

In a similar way, we can't trust our senses to reveal when God is working. Some of what He does can certainly be sensed, but I believe that most of what He does in our lives is completely undetected by us in the moment. We can't rely on our senses or feelings, which is why Scripture reminds us,

"For we walk by faith, not by sight" (Second Corinthians 5:7).

So what is the process? What is the plan that God is working through the worrisome seasons of our lives? How does everything that God is speaking to us through His Word come together in a systematic way that brings clarity instead of confusion and comfort instead of chaos? It's simply this—worry leads to waiting, and waiting leads to oneness.

All the Pieces Fit Together

Let's start at the very beginning and follow the process by which all these pieces fit together.

First, Jesus commands us not to worry, and so we must obey, but that does not mean there won't be worrisome situations and problems in our lives. As we encounter those scenarios, instead of submitting to a mindset of worry, we instead submit to the lordship of Christ by surrendering the situation over to Him through prayer.

Second, in a mindset of prayer, God bestows upon us a sense of peace that transcends the obvious circumstances, but the circumstances may not immediately change, so we are placed in a position of waiting. It's this very peace through prayer that allows us to continue to walk in victory over thoughts of worry and anxiety.

Finally, as we wait with expectancy and faith that God is going to move in power through our prayers, we draw closer to Him as He draws closer to us in deeper intimacy and oneness. This binding and twisting between us and God is where we delve even deeper into a oneness relationship with Him, which is the gift He wants to impart to us.

What a gift this is! To know God deeper and in an even more intimate way. For our faith to become more real, tangible, and tested. To see His power and faithfulness to bring about a good and complete work in our lives by redeeming all circumstances for His glory, even the ugly ones. And even to release us of those initial thoughts of worry and anxiety that started this whole process to begin with by literally overwhelming them with His power, purpose, and presence.

It's the reason why David could say with confidence,

"The salvation of the righteous is from the Lord; He is their strength in the time of trouble. And the Lord shall help them and deliver them…and save them, because they trust in Him" (Psalm 37:39-40).

Will you trust Him?

7

The Journey Continues

So now I sit on the other side of the fulfillment of God's promise that one day I'd be a pastor, but the journey is far from over. We've had so many ups and downs that I could write a separate book on that topic alone, along with each corresponding miracle the Lord provided.

And I have seen miracles.

Miracles Past

I remember in my adolescence there was a season of incredible spiritual growth and faith. There was a supernatural boldness and maturity that, looking back, I now realize was totally disproportionate with my age and life experience. There was a willingness to just "put myself out there" and see what might happen, and God did not disappoint. It was in the midst of that season that God spoke to me about my future calling.

In that time, I would agree to lead worship, when I barely even knew how to play the guitar. I would commit to teach the Bible, when I lacked confidence to speak in public. I would share my faith with my classmates, uncertain of whether they would receive or reject me. I would go on mission trips with my school, when I had never been outside the country with my own family.

And in the midst of all these "anxious" situations, I saw God's miracles and faithfulness abound. The stories I could tell you and the exploits I could share would shock you. They still shock me, all these years later! God moved in discernable power and I was an active and willing witness and participant.

Then I grew up, and became a "responsible" adult. I chose to play it safe, to walk the line, and follow the American dream. In doing so, I began to notice that the miracles and exploits became fewer and further between, until eventually, every time I shared a testimony about God's power, the context was in the past.

I remember even saying out loud to the Lord once, "Why did the miracles end? Why is the evidence of all Your power in the past?"

Miracles Present

Of course, that all changed when I obeyed the Lord's call to step out in faith and potentially risk everything to follow His lead. I gave away my business, quit my job, and laid myself and my family, finances, dreams, and accomplishments on the alter. This, of course, created incredible thoughts and emotions of worry and fear in my heart. So I laid those down on the alter, too.

In exchange for those items, God gave me miracles and exploits with Him again! Only they were better and sweeter this time around because now I shared the adventure with Juanita, Skylar, and Maksim. As a family, we became active and willing witnesses and participants of God's power...together.

I can't help reflecting back at the moment at the cross on the vacant Wildwood property, when I was crying out to God with all my unanswered questions.

In fear and worry I brought my uncertainties to Him. How was I supposed to pay the mortgage? Would Juanita remain supportive when life became difficult? And what about our children? Would they grow up resenting the sacrifice, and who would they blame?

In response, the Holy Spirit reminded me—*You can focus on what you don't know, or you can focus on what you do know.*

Ultimately, what I know is that God always keeps His promises. All these years later, true to His word, the Lord has provided for us financially, Juanita and I remain joyfully committed to serving Him in ministry, and Skylar and Maksim love the Lord and His people.

Looking back, the decisions I made in late 2011 and early 2012 are some of the best decisions of my life. Despite the hardships, I don't regret it. Every day, I walk in a surreal sense of purpose and joy, as I get the honor and privilege to live out my calling, with my family by my side.

Miracles Future

The potential for a bright and promising future is available for all of us, yet much of it depends on the attitude of our minds. Are we going to walk in the victory that Christ secured on the cross, or will we walk in voluntary defeat? Will we live like conquerors through Christ, or will we act like the conquered? Are we going to take our thoughts and emotions captive, or will we surrender and allow them to take us captive?

The choice is ours, yet Paul reminds us,

"Who shall separate us from the love of Christ? Shall tribulation, or distress, or persecution, or famine, or nakedness, or peril, or sword? Yet in all these things we are more than conquerors through Him who loved us" *(Romans 8:35 & 37).*

Who is more than a conqueror? We are through Christ. That's the future journey each son and daughter of God has to look forward to, if we will only walk forward in boldness and believe.

Epilogue

You may have noticed that often people use the words "worry" and "anxious" interchangeably. Anxiety, however, is something related, but different. Worry is a thought, whereas anxiety is a feeling. It could be said that worry begins in the mind and if allowed to take hold, manifests itself as anxiety in the body. Worry is not tangible, unlike anxiety which is very tangible.

The physical feelings that Pastor Andrew described earlier in the introduction of this book clearly qualify as feelings of anxiety. He described this sensation as "uncontrollable panic...sobbing, shaking, rocking, and not being able to respond to anything or anyone." Andrew was having an anxiety (panic) attack. The origin began in his mind, but it exhibited itself in a very real way through his body. Similarly, the darkness in Exodus 10:21 could also be "felt."

It's so much better if we could guard our minds so that we don't head down the road of physical symptoms. I've already stated that I believe this is one of the reasons why Scripture addresses worry so clearly, because if left unchecked, it leads to anxiety and all its ailments.

At the same time, we can reverse engineer this one step further back and observe that worry is actually based in fear. It's because of our fear that we worry (as we studied earlier with the disciples in the midst of the storm). We're afraid of rejection, so we worry about being honest and vulnerable with the people in our lives. We're afraid of failure, so we worry about following our dreams or setting lofty goals. We're afraid of death, so we fill our lives with meaningless material things, to distract us from our finite mortality. Our fear leads us to worry, and worry leads us to anxiety, which further feeds the fear, and the cycle repeats over and over again.

I want to be careful to point out that I don't think fear and concern are the same thing. There are certainly scenarios that require us to be careful, cautious, and prudent. On this subject, Solomon warns us,

"The simple believes every word, but the prudent considers well his steps" (Proverbs 14:15).

Prudence is wisdom, fear is folly. Prudence is based on facts; fear is based on fiction. Prudence is based on reality; fear is based on fantasy. Biblically, there is a place for prudence, but there isn't one for fear.

This truth is clearly demonstrated when John boldly stated,

"There is no fear in love; but perfect love casts out fear" (First John 4:18).

Think about that statement. Perfect love casts out fear. There is no more perfect love than God, which means the very nature and presence of God casts out fear. In other words, God and fear cannot coexist in the same space. His very essence drives fear away.

The irony in all of this is that fear and worry are not truly real—they are only real to the extent that they exist in our minds. They are immaterial and have no true form. They only exist if we allow them to. Just as easily as they can be conjured up, they can be eliminated.

So here's the takeaway—submitting to fear and worry is a choice we *don't* have to make. Literally. We have every tool and resource at our disposal so that we don't have to crumble under their weight. Of course, this doesn't mean that difficult situations won't arise (they will), but it does mean that we have control over how we react to them.

It's like a door-to-door salesman. We can place the sign out front that says "no solicitors," but that's not going to stop them from knocking on the door. However, just because they're knocking on the door doesn't mean we need to open the door, have a conversation, and then sign on the dotted line.

The reality is, as believers in Jesus Christ, we are fighting from a place of victory, we're not fighting for victory. The war has already been won and we're on the winning team! We just need to remember that fact so that we can think like victors, so we can start living like victors.

Satan knows the causal relationship between our thoughts and actions, which is why he works overtime to defeat us in our minds. If a prisoner can somehow be convinced to believe he is still a prisoner, even if the cell door is sitting wide open, then it will make no practical difference that the door is open because in his mind the door is closed!

The finished work of the cross cannot be undone, but it can certainly be forgotten.

That's where the power and presence of God must be employed in our lives. For us to live in victory over our deceptive thoughts and emotions, we must keep our focus on the eternal picture that salvation in Christ affords us.

If fear and worry only exist in our minds, and the perfect love and presence of God casts out fear, then what we need to win the battle of our minds is to saturate our lives with a deeper knowledge and more intimate relationship with God. So we reject the lies by standing on His truth. We repel the darkness by shining His light.

This is the reason David would say,

"In Your presence is fullness of joy" (Psalm 16:11).

There's no fear in His presence, there's no worry or anxiety in His presence. Instead, there's joy and freedom! There's victory. Victory over the lies, victory over past failures, victory over the darkness, victory over our emotions…pure, unadulterated victory that can only be found in and through Jesus Christ.

My prayer for all of us is, though we can't stop the trials and tribulations in our lives, that we can stop victimizing ourselves further by falling for a lie that we are helpless bystanders in a cosmic war. We are not helpless bystanders; no, we are more than conquerors through Christ. That's who I am. That's who you are. And the sooner we start believing that, and therefore start living like that, the sooner the darkness will be swallowed up in His light.

You will keep him in perfect peace, whose mind is stayed on You, because he trusts in You.

Isaiah 26:3

Appendix

The following are questions which are intended to help you introspectively assess your own thoughts and feelings regarding the material contained in this book. I pray that these questions help bring some clarity and personalization to your own unique circumstances.

Lesson One: God Commands Us Not to Worry

1. Every one of us would say that we would choose to obey His command not to worry. What might make this difficult in the midst of a trial? What does choosing to worry actually reveal about our current walk of faith?

2. Why can we be confident, even though we are not perfect in love? What does He promise us?

3. Submission is clearly linked to lordship. What "worldly" lust and pride may enslave us and keep us from total surrender?

4. When Jesus says not to worry about our lives, He's telling us to trust Him to provide for our needs and to live with an

eternal perspective. If we've been saved to serve, what does our kingdom-mindedness look like?

5. Why are we more valuable than any of God's creations? Think about the abilities you've been gifted with and how they are to be used as we represent Him.

6. What is the interpretation of "stature" in Matthew 6:27? How pure would our motives be in desiring to add stature to our lives?

7. Nothing good comes from worry. In fact, what does our worrying actually reveal about our faith?

8. Even though Jesus' words, "O you of little faith" hit hard, why should we remain encouraged? Jesus is not condemning, but convicting us. What's the difference?

9. When Jesus rebuked the winds and the sea, He was not in a hurry. Does being in a "rush" cause fear, doubt, and worry? Is this how we elevate a minor issue into a major one?

10. Can you define omnipresence, omniscience, and omnipotence? Meditate on Proverbs 3:5-6, even verses 7 and

8. Commit yourself to the One who knows and choose faith over fear!

11. Spiritual attacks in the form of doubt, worry, and fear come from the devil. What tools have we been given to quench those fiery darts? How are we to put them on?

12. If we have all the power we need through the Holy Spirit that dwells within us, why do we open the door to the condemnation of the enemy? How strong are we in the flesh?

13. When are we susceptible to "buying lies"? How are we to be made strong in Him as a world overcomer?

14. Remember that although Jesus calmed the storm in Matthew 8, He allows others to continue. Where do we find peace in the midst of a "storm"? Can we see the gift in the trial as we're going through it?

15. From the broken toy illustration, we would be wise to cast our cares upon Him. If it's important to us, then He wants to meet that need. What keeps us from asking in faith for those needs to be met? Are some needs too big? Are others too trivial?

16. What's the key word in Matthew 7:11? It must be important since Jesus had just said it in verse 7! How do we activate our faith?

17. How should we pray in regard to our needs? We often pray, "Your will, not ours, be done." If we desire a specific outcome, are we truly walking in the wisdom of Proverbs 3:5-6?

18. Seeking the kingdom of God requires a true desire for the revelation of His righteous rule in our lives. Practically, how is this contrary to the world's perspective on meeting personal needs?

19. What is the correlation between striving to meet our needs and worry? How do we cleanse our hearts from worry?

20. Can we be susceptible to giving our problems more attention than they deserve? How can we put them in proper perspective if we do not consider the magnitude and immensity of our God? Does Genesis 1 help you begin to understand the enormity of God?

21. What is your response to someone who says that we are too reliant on God who has given us the ability to provide for ourselves?

22. Jesus told us that troubles will come. Nonetheless, why are we to be of good cheer? What praiseworthy things can you meditate on that magnify the Lord rather than your troubles?

23. The free will afforded us to surrender our lives to Jesus Christ doesn't stop at salvation. We have been set apart and must choose daily to deny ourselves and follow Him. How are you being sanctified as you submit and surrender to His lordship? How is Jesus the Lord of your life?

Lesson Two: How Do We Deal with Worry?

1. Have you ever had a good reason, perhaps as the Philippians did, to be anxious? How does choosing to stay worried affect how God wants to work in the storm?

2. What is an imperative? Why aren't these always interpreted literally as they are intended to be?

3. Any believer would agree that we should seek God in all of our decisions. What types of scenarios can cause us to

minimize His lordship? Dare I ask what would even cause us to forget about Him?

4. To what do we attribute our lack of urgency when it comes to "hurling" our burdens upon Him? Unknowingly, who do we tend to cast our cares upon before seeking the Lord?

5. We have been given opportunities to bless others with God-given provision. Can you describe the blessed joy of giving? How about the gratitude of receiving?

6. One practical way to look at Scripture can be to observe the relationship between "if" and "then" concepts. How does this apply to Philippians 4:6, regarding a cure for a spirit of fear? For example, according to this verse, if we don't want to be anxious, then what should we do?

7. A biblical truth that should bring us great rest is knowing that God knows our needs better than we do! How should that influence and possibly redirect our prayers? Are the desires of your heart aligned with His for you?

8. The Spirit yearns jealously, desiring to intimately know you and to be known by you. How is your prayer life? Is it more than asking? What's the "prize" in prayer?

9. Think of those whom you share life with. You pour out your current worries to them, while also giving God praise for fears that have been conquered. Do you have that same relationship with our Father in heaven? If not, what does He say about drawing near?

10. When has God answered your prayers even though you forgot to keep praying (more than likely, quite often)? How can meditating on His faithfulness move you from fear to faith?

11. We bring our requests to the Lord in an attitude of gratitude. How much of our prayers include praise and thanksgiving? What priority do these have in our prayers?

12. How can we balance our requests with gratitude? Have you ever heard of P.R.A.Y. and A.C.T.S.? Organize your prayers within the framework of Praise, Repent, Ask, and Yield, or Adoration, Confession, Thanksgiving and Supplication. Don't get locked in, but these might be helpful.

13. Have you ever been "stuck" in your prayers? How innumerably can you acknowledge God's blessings and promises? How have His blessings outweighed our needs?

14. God will freely give us all things that we need. Most notably is the gift of reconciliation with our holy God. What led you to accept Jesus as your Lord and Savior? What gift have we been given as assurance of our salvation?

15. We have free will as to how we respond to our circumstances. What tools have we been given to defeat worry? How do we maintain an attitude that focuses on His goodness rather than what we don't have?

16. God's faithfulness is such that He has never failed in the past, therefore, we can be confident that He will remain ever-faithful, for He cannot deny Himself. However, what can shake our confidence? How are we to delight in Him or press in?

17. How does being thankful change your perspective of and response to a trying situation? How can anxiety and doubt cause you to miss the gift in the trial?

18. The calmest part of the storm is the center or the eye. Jesus is that "eye" of the trial we're going through. What does Philippians 4:6-7 emphasize so that we will be filled with His peace?

19. It has been said that Christianity is a war to be waged, and that battle begins in the mind. What are we to do with our thought life when doubt, worry, and fear begin to creep in?

20. His peace guards our thoughts and emotions. Trusting in ourselves, how do our minds and hearts lead us? How are we unprotected when we listen to our own voice and follow our heart?

21. If we truly love the Lord with all of our thoughts and emotions, then there are many benefits, namely being filled with His peace regardless of circumstances. How is obedience, or Lordship, linked to being guarded by this supernatural peace?

22. What keeps us from praying so that the door of peace will be opened to us? Are we praying for the trial to end or for peace in the trial?

23. Is your prayer life hindered by more than Satan and his distractions? Have you allowed anything to replace your devotional time? Is there any bondage keeping you from the intimate relationship God desires to have with you?

24. In what ways is prayer a God-given tool so that we're never alone in our walk?

25. How can meditating on a few verses of Scripture be more valuable than reading through a few chapters? Better yet, how can reading the Word prayerfully enhance your meditation?

26. Meditating on positive things guards our hearts and minds, but requires effort. "Camping out" in worry and fear, past or present, seems to come much easier. Why is that? How can we replace fear with faith?

27. If you choose to worry about the unknown, what does that say about your trust and faith in God? Instead, what promises can you put your faith in?

28. The eye is the lamp for the body. What can you infer from Philippians 4:8 that you shouldn't shine any light on?

29. When it comes to worry, are you trusting in the finished work of the cross? Are your choices based on a spirit of fear or one of power, love, and a sound mind? Are you placing your focus on what you don't know, or in the One who does?

Lesson Three: A Special Gift of the Lord

1. As we put our faith in the perfect timing of God, what does waiting on the Lord look like? How are we to use the tools that have been given to us?

2. How does the biblical definition of waiting differ from the world's view? How are the flesh and the Spirit warring against each other?

3. Truth brings calm. How can Isaiah 55:8-9 help you to trust and lean on the Lord as you wait on Him in the midst of a period of uncertainty? How do these verses give you confidence?

4. Our obedience is linked to blessings. How have you been blessed when obeying His commands to "act" or "wait"? Has delayed obedience had any unfruitful outcomes?

5. Just as Job lacked understanding, we are to yield our lives to God as our Lord and Master. Is He truly the preeminence in your life? Have you given Him lordship over all, or just part of it?

6. How does being in submission to the Lord's authority benefit you in waiting with expectancy? What are we to do while we wait?

7. Although we cannot understand the things of God, we trust in Him by faith. What is your response to the world's view that we exercise "blind faith"?

8. What are the intended benefits during the process of waiting on the Lord? How are you strengthened?

9. How is God's view of waiting contrary to that of the world's?

10. The deeper meaning of words in the Bible can get lost in the translation into English. This certainly applies to the Hebrew word *qavah*. How does its original meaning bring clarity as to how we are to wait?

11. When have you waited for something eagerly with expectancy? Have you been able to repeat that same level of readiness and anticipation?

12. How does waiting properly renew your strength, give you an eternal perspective, and enable you to persevere and be made strong?

13. As you wait, is your state of expectancy in line with God's will? Would you dare to attempt to maneuver the outcome? Is your heart fully loyal to Him as you're waiting?

14. How is passive waiting linked to a worldly perspective, while *qavah* waiting is in line with an eternal one? What effect does *qavah* waiting have on worry?

15. Psalm 46:10 tells us, "Be still, and know that I am God." While being quiet, what should we be contemplating? How can this eliminate fear and keep us in perfect peace?

16. How can you get the most out of being bound and twisted together? Is waiting on the Lord only about the outcome? What is God's desire during the process of waiting?

17. Looking back upon any season of waiting, how did you take advantage of it to draw closer to God? Conversely, did you resist the gift of oneness that He intended? How so?

18. Now that you know that waiting brings oneness, how does this affect your prayer life, fellowship with brethren, and how you are to serve within the body? Is God working behind the scenes by Himself? What is your part?

19. The abundant life that Jesus promised is a life full of experiences designed to create oneness with Him. During anxious times how should we pray, being bound and twisted together, replacing fear with faith?

20. What choices do you have during a prolonged season of waiting? What is God's will for you during that season?

21. Amongst believers there is not to be an expectation of avoiding worrisome situations (John 16:33). So how are obedience and lordship linked to overcoming worry?

22. How does Isaiah 26:3 apply to waiting on Him in oneness? Why is prayer so vital to tapping in to His peace?

23. God promises that as we submit to Him and draw near, He draws closer to us (James 4:7-8). Knowing that faith requires action, how can you exercise your faith today to draw near to Him? He has a gift of intimacy for you.

24. Philippians 1:6 reminds us, "He who has begun a good work in you will complete it." During this process are you willing to trust and obey Him so that you may receive the gift He so freely gives—Himself?

Acknowledgments

A special thanks to Alicia Evans for carefully reading over this manuscript, making edits, and offering suggestions for improvement. You have been such an answer to prayer. Thank you for making my writing better.

Thanks also to John Hardin for taking the time to write each lesson's follow-up questions. Your humility and willingness to serve the Lord are an example and testimony to all who have the privilege of knowing you.

As always, thank you, Michelle Vicario, for being the best assistant a pastor could ask for. Your help transcribing the follow-up questions was truly a blessing.

Last but never least, thank you Pastor Andrew Enos for your constant friendship and faithfulness all these years. None of my writing would even exist if it weren't for your perpetual encouragement and accountability.

About the Author

Erik V. Sahakian has committed his life to serving Jesus Christ through teaching God's inerrant Word, ministering to the body of Christ, and writing. He joyfully worships and serves with his wife and children at Wildwood Calvary Chapel in Yucaipa, CA.

Visit www.eriksahakian.com to learn more.

Made in the USA
Middletown, DE
27 May 2019